As Curator of the Carisbrooke Castle Museum, Roy Brinton is an acknow-
ledged authority on the history of the Isle of Wight. He was born on the
Island, and joined the local history staff of the Isle of Wight County Council in
1978. He is well-known for his lectures on the Ryde area and as the author of
several books on old Isle of Wight illustrations, amongst them *Edwardian
Island*, the companion volume to *Victorian Island*.

1. *(Following page)* The Diamond Jubilee of Queen Victoria was
celebrated enthusiastically on the Island during June and July 1897.
The Queen paid official visits to Newport, Ryde and Cowes.
A dinner was given in celebration at the Town Hall, Ryde, and the
local Court photographer, Gustav Mullins, presented copies
of this portrait of the Queen as a souvenir.

VICTORIAN ISLAND

The Isle of Wight in Victorian Photographs

ROY BRINTON

THE DOVECOTE PRESS

This book is dedicated to the memory of Rod Oliver;
a good friend who loved the Island and its history.

First published in 1994 by the Dovecote Press Ltd
Stanbridge, Wimborne, Dorset BH21 4JD

Text © Roy Brinton 1994

Designed by the Dovecote Press Ltd
Photoset by The Typesetting Bureau, Wimborne, Dorset
Printed and bound in Singapore.

ISBN 1 874336 28 8

Contents

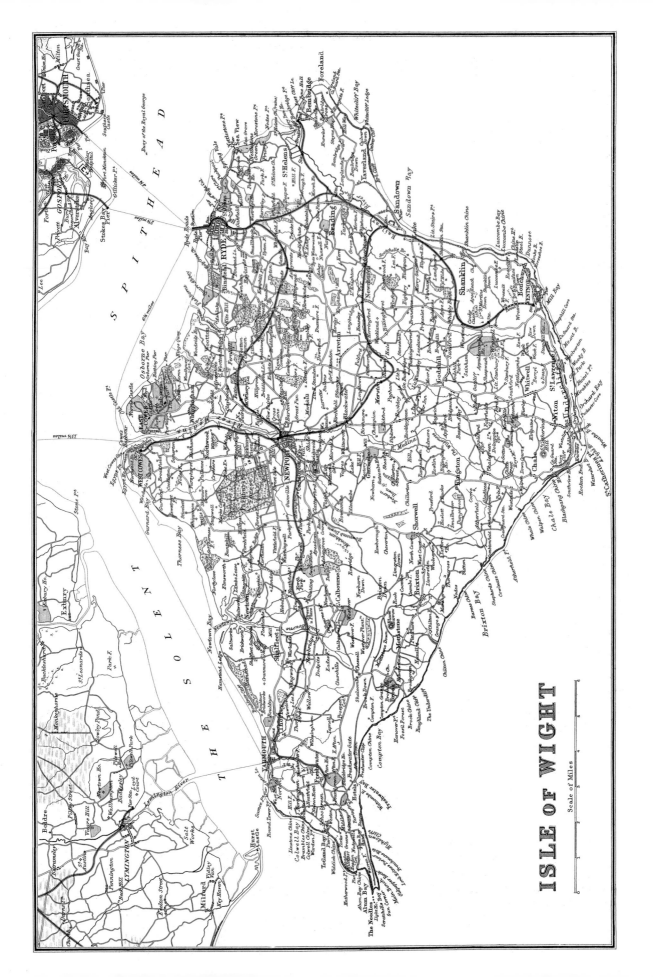

ISLE OF WIGHT

Scale of Miles

Introduction

In the early 19th century the Isle of Wight saw a change in its economy with a move from being dependent entirely on agriculture to a mixture of tourism and agriculture.

The first visitors to tour the Island were the gentry, who, bringing their own coaches, started to arrive in the second half of the 18th century. This arrival was the result of improvements to mainland roads, better designed coaches and a more frequent ferry service across the Solent. With these improvements travellers started to include the Isle of Wight in their tours of the southern half of England in search of 'picturesque' and romantic scenery.

There was a choice of ferry routes across the Solent. The Southampton to Cowes route was the most popular, partly because Southampton was a more attractive port to visit and an easier landing was to be made at Cowes. The next favoured route was from Portsmouth to Ryde, but landing had to be made on the open beach at Ryde.

In the early 19th century all of the public roads on the Island came under the control of one authority, and this led to great improvements to the main roads and to the building of new ones. The time taken was shortened and the comfort of crossing the Solent from Portsmouth to Ryde greatly improved with the building of Ryde Pier in 1814 and the introduction of regular steam packets in 1825.

The railway from London reached Southampton in 1840 and in the September of the following year the directors of the Southampton Railway organised the first day return trip from London, leaving at 6.50 a.m. for Southampton; a cruise round the Island, back to Southampton and returning to London, arriving at 9.35 that evening, all at a total cost of £1. This trip was repeated the following May. By 1849 the railway was organising day trips which allowed six hours on the Island.

Public transport did not exist on the Isle of Wight until the first stage coaches started to run from Cowes to Newport in 1770, and gradually services spread until all the towns and villages were linked. The early visitors had to stay either in the small inns or rent cottages, but in the early 19th century many inns carried out enlargements and offered increased comforts. Hotels started to be built, such as the 'Marine' at Cowes and 'Yelfs' at Ryde. In 1862 the first railway was built on the Island, running from Cowes to Newport and two years later another was opened from Ryde to Shanklin and later extended to Ventnor. This railway connected the main resorts and was soon moving large numbers of visitors.

As the 19th century progressed wealth increased and the standard of living rose. The 1861 census recorded for the first time an excess of urban over rural population. These two factors meant that many more people could take advantage of modern travel and get away from the cities and into the countryside or to the seaside.

More visitors led to the demand for information and various forms of guide books started to appear. The first Island guide was published in 1794 by Henry Wyndham, with the author suggesting inns at which to stay, transport that could be hired and daily tours that might be made. In the 1830s local authors and printers, such as Brannon, started to produce pocket size guide books illustrated with engravings of Island scenes.

Photography, which had started some ten years earlier, underwent an important change in the early 1850s. A new process called collodion or 'wet plate' was developed. Using a sheet of coated glass as a negative it was possible to produce a much sharper print than before. The main disadvantage was that the plates had to be prepared, exposed and processed all within a few minutes. Therefore photographers working out of doors had to take along a portable dark-room. This new process meant that mass production of prints was now possible and the cost of individual prints was very much cheaper. This led to a fashionable new way of using photographic views on visiting card size mounts.

2. Jabez Hughes came to Ryde in 1861 when he purchased the photographic business of William Lacy, The Arcade, Union Street. By March 1863 he was receiving commissions from Queen Victoria and other members of the Royal family.

3. Tom Piper was born in 1876, the son of William Piper, a Newport hawker who sold souvenirs outside the gates of Carisbrooke Castle. Tom became a photographer and sold photographs of both the interior and exterior of the Castle.

The 1870s brought another sweeping change to the process of photography. By using new materials and equipment it was possible to do away with the need to prepare plates in advance. Prepared plates, and films, could be bought in the shops. Cameras continued to be improved and some new ones could be hand held. All of this resulted in ordinary people being able to practice photography for themselves, and the range of pictures taken became much more varied.

Many of the first Island photographic views were taken by visiting mainland photographers such as Russell Sedgefield and Frank Good. Their work appeared in the form of 21 hand mounted photographs in the book *The Isle of Wight* by J. Redding Ware, (1869). However resident photographers were also producing views and one of the first was James Briddon who had 20 of his views published in 1866 in *The History of the Isle of Wight* by George Henry Venables. Other Island photographers, such as John Symonds and James Beading were producing views on visiting card size mounts. As the century progressed the Island became the home of many professional photographers, ranging from Jabez Hughes who arrived on the Island in 1861 and became a leading court photographer, to Joseph Milman Brown who started in Shanklin in 1868 and became a well known landscape photographer, winning prizes in London, Paris and Vienna. Another example of the variety of photographers was Tom Piper who appears to have only photographed in and around Carisbrooke Castle.

My thanks go to those Victorian photographers who produced such good quality work that has survived to the present day. In *Victorian Island* I have used some examples of their art in an attempt to show what the Isle of Wight was like in the last half of the 19th century.

I am indebted to Miss Yvonne Arthur, Mrs Pam Matheson, Mr Raymond Weeks and Carisbrooke Castle Museum for kindly allowing me to use examples from their photographic collections. My thanks are also due to my wife for checking the text and Mrs Jo Barry for typing it.

ROY BRINTON, *Ryde*.

Ryde

4. The Esplanade in the early 1870s. In the centre of the photograph is the Esplanade Hotel which opened in 1867 and on the extreme left are the docks, which were built in 1859 and filled in twenty years later.

5. The railway pier at Ryde was opened in 1880. It was built to run parallel to the tramway pier. This photograph shows the new Ryde Esplanade Station. Near the crane on the quay are two of the towboats used to bring goods over from the mainland.

6. 'The Elms' was built in High Park Road, Ryde in the latter part of the century and was occupied by Major Peter Crawford and his wife. The house stood in a half acre of ground planted with trees and shrubs and included a croquet lawn.

7. An interior view of the milking parlour of Stainer's Dairy, which was situated to the rear of the High Street, near Well Street. The cows were grazed in fields to the south of the town and driven in each day to be milked.

8. This class photograph is typical of many taken in the latter part of the 19th century. Bettesworth Road School, Ryde, was built by the local school board in 1877 for 570 children.

9. There were several brickworks in the Ryde area and this photograph shows the brickmaker holding a mould as he and his lad prepare green bricks for firing. The horse would have worked the pugmill.

10. The bow-fronted Brougham was a very popular carriage for hire. Many of Ryde's wealthier inhabitants wanted to enjoy the benefits of a carriage, but not the expense of keeping their own – hence the popularity of livery stables which hired out carriages by the day.

11. Horse drawn water carts were often seen in Ryde, especially in summer when they sprayed the streets to keep the dust down. During one summer drought the Council tried spraying the streets with sea water, but all their equipment became corroded.

12. The mounted band of the Hampshire Carabineers in Swanmore Road in July 1899. They had attended Queen Victoria at the Royal Isle of Wight County Hospital when she opened the new Children's Wing.

13. Upton windmill was probably the largest windmill on the Island, being some six floors high. On the extreme right is the stump of an earlier mill built in the early 19th century and the large mill replaced it later in the same century.

14. This thatched cottage stood at the south end of Swanmore Road, by the junction with Ashey Road. It was demolished towards the end of the century.

15. John Grist opened the Upper West Street post office, Ryde, in 1874. One of his duties was the delivery of the mail, and in this late 19th century photograph he is in Mitchells Road, Haylands, before going on to Havenstreet.

16. *(Below)* Ryde Pier, one of the earliest in England, was constructed in 1814-15. The tramway pier, left of the pedestrian one, was built in 1864 to convey passengers in comfort from the boats to the shore. A tram car can be seen in the siding.

17. *(Right)* One of Mr F Bradley's steam tram engines. Two were built in 1880 for use on the Ryde Pier Tramway, but they did not prove to be a great success and were withdrawn from service a few years later. This photograph was taken at Ryde St John's Depot in about 1885.

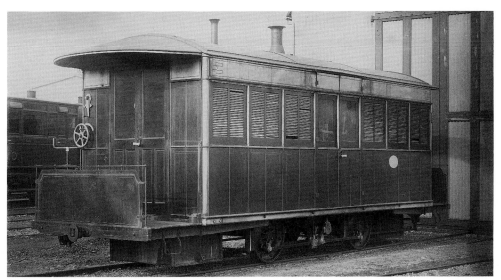

18. In January 1881, during a furious snowstorm and gale, two colliers, the *Havelock* and the *John Warder* were driven against the new Ryde railway pier. A section of about 100 yards of the pier was carried away, involving thousands of pounds worth of damage.

19. Ryde Pier Head with the *Princess Margaret* alongside. She was built in 1893 to carry 472 passengers on the Ryde to Portsmouth route. Approaching the pier is the Southampton based *Duchess of York* which was built in 1896.

20. The High Street shop of John Purnell decorated for the Diamond Jubilee of Queen Victoria. Purnells were a well-known furnishing and undertaking business. The 'Singer' shop on the left stands on the corner of the High Street and Garfield Road.

21. This floral arch was erected on Ryde Esplanade in July 1874 to commemorate the arrival of Queen Victoria's eldest daughter, the Crown Princess of Prussia and her husband. The arch was covered in evergreens and the shields of Britain and Prussia, also the motto *Gott Mit Uns* (God with us).

Brading

22. This is the bull-ring in the centre of Brading, with the actual ring just visible in the road to the right of the ladies. The old stone and brick-built malt house was later demolished and left as an open space.

23. The main street in Brading showing the Red Lion Inn on the left.

24. This photograph was taken about 1882 and shows an exposed part of flooring at the Roman villa, near Brading. It was later covered with a roof and became part of the main shed covering the villa.

25. The main drive and parkland of Nunwell House, seen in the distant centre. The Nunwell estate, near Brading, had been in the possession of the Oglander family for several hundred years and was visited by Charles I when he was at Carisbrooke Castle.

26. It is thought that Binstead Church was erected in Norman times to serve local quarry workers. In 1844 the old nave was demolished and replaced by the one seen in this photograph. It was designed by Thomas Hellyer in the Early English Style.

27. *(Below)* In the 19th century parts of the medieval ruins of Quarr Abbey were adapted to form a gothic style farmhouse, with a barn behind. A thatched cattle shelter can be seen amid the ruins. This area was very popular with Victorians walking out from Ryde.

28. *(Opposite top)* The medieval site of Quarr Abbey was excavated in 1891 under the supervision of a local architectural historian, Percy Stone. This view shows some of the walls of the *frater* or refectory. In the centre is the blocked serving hatch leading through to the kitchen beyond and in the foreground the undercroft of the *dorter* or dormitory is being excavated.

29. *(Opposite below)* Princess Beatrice married Prince Henry of Battenberg in 1885 and they spent the first two days of their marriage at Quarr Abbey House, near Ryde. The Newport photographer, Charles Knight, has superimposed a photograph of the couple on to a photograph of the house to produce a honeymoon portrait.

30. The tide mill at Wootton Bridge originally belonged to Quarr Abbey. It was enlarged several times during its long history and when this photograph was taken the miller was William Souter. The spritsail barge *Edith* has crossed from the mainland and is trying to get alongside the mill quay, despite the ice in this wintry photograph.

31. This decorated arch was erected by a local committee across the road at Wootton Bridge in 1885 to celebrate the wedding of Princess Beatrice. The couple passed under the arch on their way to Quarr Abbey House.

St Helens & Bembridge

32. Brading Harbour was finally enclosed in 1880 by the Brading Harbour Improvement & Railway Co. The railway line from Brading to St Helens had been completed three years earlier. When this photograph was taken in 1879, the sluices near St Helens Quay were being constructed. In the left background can be seen the open doors of the engine shed and to the right a vertical steam boiler and a four-wheeled carriage.

33. Colonel Augustus Moreton (1848-1918) of Hillgrove, Bembridge, had a son who was killed in the First World War, and seven daughters. He had Duice Avenue laid out and built a home for each of his daughters. It is possibly some of those children that we see here with their nannies.

34. *(Left)* Bembridge Windmill is a typical example of an 18th century stone built tower mill. When the miller, who in the late 19th century was Robert Tuffley, wished to work the mill, he would have covered the wooden sails with sail cloth.

35. *(Below)* The paddle steamer *Island Queen* was built in Port Glasgow and went into service on the Portsmouth to Bembridge route in 1882. She stayed for 16 years and then was sold to a firm in Gibraltar. The Royal Spithead Hotel was also completed in 1882 at a cost of about £10,000.

Sandown

36. This is a typical beach scene at Sandown in the 1880s with the bathing machines to the left. They belonged to Silas Southcott, who also had a lodging house in the High Street. In the background is the pier before it was extended in 1895.

37. *(Opposite top)* Sandown Pier was opened by the Sandown Pier Co. in 1876 to a length of 350 feet. After nine years the Company failed and the pier was put up for auction. The new owners decided to lengthen it to about 900 ft and to erect a pavilion on a new pier head. This work was completed in September 1895. The steamer approaching is the *Dandie Dinmont*.

38. *(Opposite below)* An early photograph of St John's Church, which was built 1880-81 and consecrated in October 1881. It was designed in the Early English Style, by Mr C Luck of London to seat 600.

39. *(Above)* The great snowstorm that swept the south of England in January 1881 was severely felt in the Island. This photograph, taken at the junction of Melville Street and High Street, shows how much snow fell.

Shanklin

Lake Toll Bar.

40. Turnpike and toll houses started to appear on the Island in 1813 as the result of the setting up of the Highway Commissioners. They were abolished in 1889. A two horse coach cost 6d, with a double charge on a Sunday. This toll gate at Lake was set up in the second half of the century.

41. Tower Cottage was built about 1825 on the edge of Shanklin Chine by General Viney. This photograph, taken some 40 years later when it was occupied by a Mrs Cameron, shows the attractive garden.

42. Five years after this building was erected as a lodging house in 1834 by Jeremiah Raynor it was sold for £1,000 to Messrs Cooper and Daish. By the time this picture was taken in about 1860 it had become known as Daish's Hotel and was managed by William Hollier.

43. *(Above)* This fine hay-making scene was taken some years before the 17th century manor house in Shanklin was rebuilt in 1883.

44. *(Left)* This posed photograph of Victorian children was taken at the foot of the old sea wall. The boats belonged to John Prouten and Alfred Colenutt.

45. This sadly rather poor quality view of the Plough & Barleycorn Inn, North Street, was taken in about 1865 when Joseph Kent was the landlord. He died in the late 1870s and his widow then became the landlady.

46. Note the man on the roof, about to carry out a much needed repair to the thatch to this old stone built cottage. In the background, to the right, is the Congregational Church, first founded in 1843 and rebuilt in 1883.

47. Taken about 1878, this photograph of Shanklin Village shows the newly established grocery business of Dear & Thomas. The large building in the background is Holliers Hotel, which was built in 1824 by William Williams, formerly a farmer in the area.

48. The railway from Ryde to Shanklin was opened in 1864 and two years later extended to Ventnor. As more railways were opened on the Island, many stage coaches became redundant. Some were broken up, but others were used to take visitors on trips to places that were not conveniently reached by the trains.

49. *(Opposite top)* This photograph, taken in about 1860 of a pair of cottages in Shanklin, clearly shows the style of clothing worn. The old man wearing a 'stove pipe' hat standing outside his front door and the smartly dressed children are all posing for the photographer.

50. *(Opposite below)* The farmer and his family outside their home, Upper Hyde Farm House. This 1870s picture shows a typical Island stone and brick built farmhouse.

51. The first railway on the Island was from Cowes to Newport and opened in 1862. Two year later the next line opened from Ryde to Shanklin and here is the first train to arrive at Shanklin. The driver was known as 'Hell-fire Jack'. The station was then a terminus but two years later the line was extended to Ventnor.

52. Bathing machines were a very important part of any seaside resort in the 19th century. This photograph taken at the foot of the Chine in about 1880, shows those belonging to two firms. Charles Moorman was one of the first suppliers and he was joined by Edward Blew in about 1875. Between two of the machines is the horse used to move them to and from the water's edge.

Bonchurch & Ventnor

53. This is an early photograph of the centre of the small village of Bonchurch, and on the right is the local builder's yard. The large blocks of stone, which were quarried locally, were probably to be used in building further villas in the area. Bonchurch's population rose from 146 in 1831, to 641 in 1871.

54. Cook's Castle was erected in the 18th century as a romantic ruin to be viewed from Appuldurcombe House across the valley. During part of the 19th century Cook's Castle was occupied by W. Fulford who served refreshments in the surrounding garden.

55. In the early 1880s the grocer Robert Barnicle started a business in Horseshoe Bay, Bonchurch, operating bathing machines and baths. His premises can be seen behind the bathing machines and the horse and carriage.

56. At 48 feet long and 12 feet wide, the old Norman church of St Boniface at Bonchurch is one of the smallest parish churches in the Island. This photograph shows the old style high sided pews and a gallery at the east end. Note also the 'tortoise' stove to heat the church and the 18th century hat pegs on both side walls.

59. *(Above)* The esplanade was built across Ventnor Cove between 1848 and 1850. This photograph, which was taken in about 1864, shows the bathing machines operated by Jacob Barton and Thomas Harding. The machines were drawn across the beach by windlasses. The very small pebbles picked up on the beach were called 'Isle of Wight Diamonds' because of their brilliancy.

57. *(Opposite top)* The railway line from Ryde reached Ventnor in 1866, and the photograph shows a passenger train alongside the new platform. The station buildings are still being erected. The engineers had tunnelled the line through the Down and brought the line into an old quarry.

58. *(Opposite below)* Ventnor railway station in about 1880, clearly showing the rail layout. On the island platform is the gangway used to enable passengers to cross over to the main platform. To the left on the side of the shed, is an advertisement for the local coal merchant, Henry Owen. His stores were at the station and his office was in the High Street.

60. Here we see the two piers - east (just visible in the top left) and west — which formed Ventnor Harbour. The Ventnor Harbour company was established by the Ventnor Harbour Act, 1862, but the company failed and the whole project went up for auction in July 1866. The following winter gales badly damaged the piers and they were sold for scrap in February 1867.

61. The Royal National Hospital for Consumption was started with a pair of houses for male patients in November 1869 and by 1877 eight pairs were built and occupied. Upon receipt of a large bequest a further three blocks were added. The chapel, on the extreme right, was built in 1871-72 with the foundation stone being laid by Bishop Wilberforce of Winchester.

62. Holy Trinity Church, with its 160 foot spire was erected to the design of a West Country architect C.E. Giles and the entire cost was met by the three daughters of Bishop Percy. The church was consecrated in August 1862. The large house with open ground in front, to the right of the spire, is Church Hill House, built as a private residence in the 1870s.

63. A rare stereoscopic photograph of St Catherine's, the first modern lighthouse to be built on the Island. It was designed by Messrs Walker & Burgess of London and built 1838-40 by Dashwoods of Ryde, at a cost of about £13,000. Its foundations are 27 feet deep and 30 feet in diameter. It was originally built to a height of 142 feet, as seen in this photograph, but because the light was often encompassed by fog the tower was lowered to 86 feet in 1875.

64. In 1869 the post office was granted a monopoly of the telegraph business in Britain. During the following year a telegraph office was opened in the High Street, Ventnor. It was under the control of George Burt, postmaster, and was open from 7.00 a.m. to 8.00 p.m. This photograph of the telegram boy was taken in the 1880s by a local photographer, John E. Briddon.

65. This is the old Niton to Blackgang road with the postman on his rounds at Rocken End. Although this section was desolate there were several large houses on the route, including 'Sandrock' at the Blackgang end, where a letter box had to be emptied twice a day.

66. To reach Blackgang Chine the visitor had to pass through the toy shop or bazaar, which was owned and managed by the Dabell family. Visitors came in great numbers, as is shown in this early Victorian photograph. Whilst a beautiful and exciting place to visit in summer, it was dangerous in winter, with gales causing several shipwrecks on the shore below the Chine.

West Wight

67. The 900 ton *Underlay* was only six years old when she became a total wreck on rocks between Luccombe and Bonchurch on the night of 25th/26th September 1871. She was carrying 30 emigrants and £30,000 worth of cargo. The iron ship was driven broadside onto the shore and could not be saved. All the passengers and crew were saved except the steward, who was drowned trying to save his canary.

68.   The German luxury liner *Eider* went aground in thick fog on the Atherfield Ledge on 31st January 1892.
She was carrying 227 passengers and 167 crew; plus 500 bags of mail. In her vault was £300,000 of bullion.
At first the Captain declined to be rescued by the local lifeboat thinking the liner would float off at high tide
but, when a severe gale blew up the rescue operation got underway. It was completely successful with the
passengers, crew, mail bags and bullion all being brought ashore.

69.   The first lifeboat stations on the Island were at Brook and Brighstone; both being opened in 1860. This
photograph shows the newly arrived boat *Worcester Cadet* at Brighstone, which was the second on the station.
The 34 foot self-righting boat arrived in August 1880, and her first rescue was in the following January, when
she went to the aid of the *S.S. Claremont*.

70, 71 These two views of Alum Bay, taken in the 1860s, show that visitors were already enjoying the beach. Most of them came to look at, and take away, samples of the richly coloured sands, for which the Bay was famous. These sands were brought to the notice of the public by Edward Dore of Newport who used them to create small pictures of Island scenes.

72, 73 & 74. The poet, Alfred Tennyson first visited the Island in 1846. Later in 1853 he came to live at Farringford House, Freshwater, and liked it enough to purchase the estate some three years later. The portrait of him was taken in 1869 by Julia Margaret Cameron. She was a famous pioneer in art photography, who came to live nearby in 1860. The rustic bridge enabled Tennyson to cross a public lane in private, from one part of his estate to another.

75. In the 18th century a lighthouse was erected on the Downs above the Needles, but because of its height was of little service in hazy and foggy weather. Trinity House therefore decided in 1859 to build a new one on the outer rock of the Needles. The building stone was brought over from Portland and landed at Totland Bay, where it was cut and dressed. It was then transported in lighters to the temporary pier, shown in the stereoscope, which had been built onto the newly cut shelf on the outer rock.

76. Totland Bay Pier was erected in 1880 and was owned by the Totland Hotel & Pier Co. The iron pier was 450 feet long and was popular in the summer with vessels calling from Bournemouth and Lymington.

77. The Totland Bay Hotel was built at the same time and by the same company as the pier in 1880. The hotel became so popular that it was enlarged in about 1885, when the tower was also added.

78. The toll bridge linking Yarmouth to Norton across the River Yar was begun in 1858 and opened to traffic in 1860. Its construction had been bitterly resented by local mariners as it restricted access to the river. Tolls charged ranged from carriages paying 6d to a mule 1d. The framers of the Act authorizing the bridge were far-sighted in enforcing a toll of 2s 6d for conveyances using steam or means other than animal.

79. A print from an early if damaged glass plate negative of the old 'Sun Inn' at Calbourne cross roads before it was destroyed by fire in April 1894. The fire was started by a lamp in a bedroom which set light to the thatch. It was quickly extinguished, but broke out again next day and this time destroyed the inn. It was later rebuilt after the local authority had realigned the roads.

Carisbrooke & Newport

80. The junction of Spring Lane (right) with Castle Hill in the latter part of the 19th century. This hill was the main approach for visitors to Carisbrooke Castle. On the left is an area known as the Shrubbery, planted in the 18th century to the orders of Lord Bolton, Governor of the Isle of Wight.

81. This photograph of Carisbrooke Castle taken by a local photographer, Tom Piper, shows the window of the room in which Princess Elizabeth died in September 1650, aged 14. The Princess died within three weeks of arrival at the Castle, and was buried in St Thomas's Church, Newport. Donkeys were in use drawing water from the well by the late 17th century and visiting Victorians enjoyed watching them at work.

82. The Isle of Wight Militia Artillery had their first headquarters at Parkhurst Barracks, but moved to Carisbrooke Castle. There, under the command of Col. Leopold Paget, they trained for 28 days each year using the cannons on the Castle's bastions. In 1885 the Militia Artillery moved to Sandown.

83. The 'Castle Hotel', on the extreme right, was in the 1870s named 'Carisbrooke Castle Hotel', with William Cantelo as landlord. About 1877 the front of the building was altered and bay windows were added on the first floor and Thomas Bungay became landlord. The next building to the left was the 'Red Lion' inn.

84. Before 1896 mentally ill people on the Island who had been certified insane were cared for at the Hampshire Asylum at Knowle. In 1891 the Island County Council was approached to build a local asylum, and in the following year a 50 acre site at Whitecroft Farm was purchased. In 1894 building commenced and two years later the first patients moved in.

85. The view looking down from the Castle walls onto the village of Carisbrooke. In the centre is the parish church of St Mary. The Norman priory which was on the northern side of the church was demolished in the 16th century. To the right of the church is the lane which went to the station on the Freshwater to Newport railway.

86. A typical Victorian portrait, posed against a painted backcloth. Jane Porter was born in 1825, the daughter of a pastry-cook who had a shop in the High Street, Newport. She married Edwin Upward, a bookseller and toy dealer who had a shop at 52 High Street. In the late 1850s he moved his business into his father-in-law's former shop. Jane died on 6 September 1866, aged 41.

87. A floral arch erected at the junction of Castle Road (left) and Carisbrooke Road (right) to commemorate the Golden Jubilee of Queen Victoria. In the centre is the memorial to Sir John Simeon who died in March 1870. On the extreme left is the grocers, wine merchants and 'Falcon Inn' all managed by William Hogg.

88. Newport Grammar School for boys was founded in the early years of the 17th century by local gentry and administered by the Corporation. In this building, on 18 September 1648, Charles I met the Parliamentary Commissioners to negotiate the treaty of Newport. The King was on parole from Carisbrooke Castle and stayed in Newport until 30 November, when he was taken away to Hurst Castle.

89. In the early 19th century the Grammar School had free places for 15 boys, sons of poor tradesmen and others of the town, but by the time this photograph was taken in 1875 the number had risen to 20 (maybe the lads without mortar boards). Fee paying boarders were also taught. The headmaster in the centre is the Rev. Edward Watts, who held the position from 1872 to 1887.

90. The bridge in this photograph carried the railway line from Newport Station across the River Medina. The signal box controlled the moveable section of the bridge which allowed vessels to reach the upper reaches of the river. The *Ellen* of Cowes, did work for Arnell Bros., millers of Mill Street, Newport. The *Hester* had Captain Matthews as master owner and he did work for J. Thomas & Co., millers.

91. A slightly faded photograph of Newport harbour in the 1880's. For hundreds of years the harbour had been the main port of import and export of goods for the Island. The original quays were at the foot of Quay Street, but during the 19th century, as business increased, so the quays were extended northwards on both sides of the river. Boat building was also carried out on the west bank.

92. The Newport (Blue) Girl's Charity School in Lugley Street was founded in 1761, for the purpose of clothing a number of poor girls of Newport, introducing them in religion and training them as domestic servants or to be apprentices. In the 19th century the school had places for 20 girls to be educated, including seven or eight who were boarders in the schoolmistress's house.

93. The Worsley Almshouse in Crocker Street was founded in 1618 by Sir Richard Worsley in pursuance of the will of Giles Kent. The Almshouse, consisting of six small tenements of one room each with a lean-to behind and a garden, was home to six poor widows of the Borough of Newport.

94. The cattle or beast market had been in St James's Square since the 12th century. When this photograph was taken in the late 19th century the market was held every Saturday and alternate Wednesdays. In the background centre is the 'Bugle Inn'. In Stuart times it was called the 'Bull' and was occupied by the Parliamentary Commissioners whilst they negotiated the treaty of Newport with Charles I.

95. Newport Town Hall was erected in 1818. It was designed by John Nash and cost £10,000. On the first floor were two handsome rooms and every Saturday a butter market was held on the ground floor. On the 28th June 1887 the foundation stone of the clock tower was laid as the Golden Jubilee Memorial to Queen Victoria.

96. On 22 July 1887 Queen Victoria visited Newport as part of her Golden Jubilee celebrations. The Mayor, flanked by the Town Clerk and the Town Sergeant, welcomed the Queen to the town. To mark the occasion a knighthood was conferred on the Mayor, Francis Pittis. The building to the left is the Isle of Wight Literary Institution which was built of Swanage stone in 1810, at a cost of £3,000. It had a newsroom and a library.

97. The timber framed 'Hare & Hounds Inn' stood on the corner of St James's Square and Upper Pyle Street. The landlord was William Yelf when it was closed in 1890. The Corporation purchased the site, demolished the inn and erected a Corn Exchange.

98. Coppins Bridge was widened in 1828 to handle the increased traffic, such as stage coaches. On the left are the timber framed 'Globe Cottages', of which the western end was at one time the 'Globe Inn'. The railway bridge, which carried the Sandown to Newport line, was erected in 1879. In the background behind the children, is the 'White Lion', which was one of five public houses in the area.

99. This photograph, taken by the Court photographers, Hughes and Mullins, is of Queen Victoria in her garden carriage. During her summer stay the Queen would use it to drive about the grounds. The carriage was built by Richard Chiverton, the coach builder of Lugley Street, Newport.

102. *(Above)* Queen Victoria purchased the Osborne estate in 1845 and a new house was built on the site of the old Georgian mansion. The Queen always regarded Osborne as her country home and would have a marquee erected for great occasions. The marquee was later replaced by a large hall in 1890. The Durbar Room, as the hall was named, was built after this photograph was taken, to the right of the Royal Apartments.

101. *(Opposite below)* Queen Victoria seen arriving at Whippingham Church for the wedding of her youngest daughter, Princess Beatrice to Prince Henry of Battenberg on 23rd July 1885.

100. *(Opposite top)* The original Whippingham Church was a small medieval building which was altered and greatly enlarged in 1804 by John Nash. Prince Albert decided that a more splendid church was needed and in 1854 had a new chancel built. The rest of the building was replaced in 1860 and 1861 and the newly completed church was opened in January 1862.

103. Medina Road decorated for the Diamond Jubilee celebrations in 1897. The Medina Commercial Wharf in Medina Road was built in the early 19th century and a pier added to reach deep water in the 1850s. A newspaper report in 1877 said that the wharf was extremely busy with some vessels unloading and having their cargo stored before going to be repaired. When this photograph was taken the agents were Robert H. Matthews & Co., who also managed the Medina Coal Co.

104. Three weeks before the death of the Queen on 22nd January 1901, Field Marshal Earl Roberts landed at East Cowes and received a public welcome outside the Town Hall. He had returned from a successful campaign in South Africa and was on his way to Osborne to be received by the Queen.

105. The carriage is passing a sentry on duty outside the main gate to East Cowes Barracks in Medina Road. During the Queen's residence at Osborne a detachment of soldiers from Parkhurst Barracks were quartered at East Cowes Barracks.

106. In 1859 the Cowes Ferry Company took over the Cowes to East Cowes crossing from John Roberton, whose family had held the right of ferry for a hundred years. The Ferry Company introduced a steam chain ferry with a passenger fare of one penny which was later reduced to ½d.

107. The Hampshire Carbineers landing at East Cowes from the steam chain ferry. They are possibly on their way to Osborne to perform ceremonial duties for the Queen.

108. The Marine Hotel, Cowes, was one of the first hotels on the Island and was very fashionable throughout the century. Famous guests included Napoleon III, who took over a whole floor when staying there in 1871. In the early 19th century the landlord would fly a flag if he had rooms available and strike it if full.

Villages & Country Scenes

109. The old parish of Newchurch was one of the largest in the Island, stretching from Ryde to Ventnor, but as the two towns grew, the parish was divided into three. The church dates from the 12th century with many alterations and additions. The thatched cottage next to the church was later demolished and replaced by a parish hall. To the right is the local hostelry, the 'Pointer's Inn'.

110, 111. The village of Arreton had two hostelries, both in the main street. One was the 'White Lion' which was near the church, and was a stage coach stop. Dashwood's Brewery was in Trafalgar Road, Newport. The house appears to have been unpopular with landlords in the 1880s as it had five in ten years. The second was the 'Red Lion', seen in the alas faded lower photograph.

112, 113. A guide book writer of 1860 said, "There are few prettier villages than Godshill to be seen anywhere in England". It was certainly popular with visitors, who were recommended to stay at the local inn, 'The Griffin'. Visits to the fine church on the hill and the 17th century grammar school were suggested. The lower photograph was taken in the 1870's and shows some cottages in the village, and their occupiers.

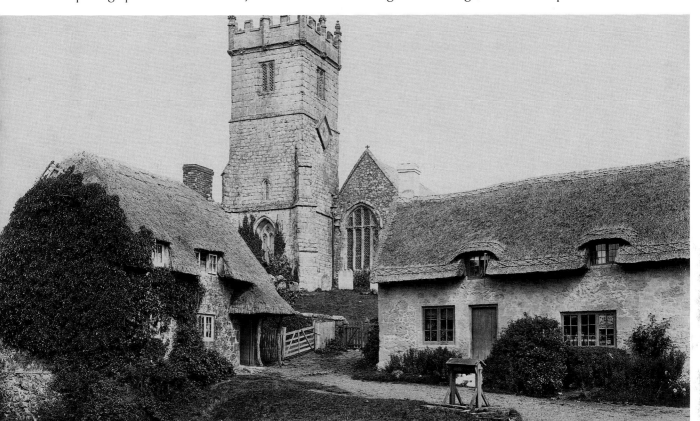

114. *(Left)* The shepherd stood apart from his fellows, enjoying special privileges throughout the centuries. He was more of an individual than other agricultural workers, with his remote sheep-fold, and wheeled cabin containing a medicine chart and an assortment of tackle and tools. Here we see him cradling a lamb and holding his neck crook, which was second only in importance to his dog.

115. *(Below)* The carriage in the photograph has just passed over the single arch bridge that crosses the Cal Bourne at Shalfleet, where the stream flows north to form the Newtown River. The shingled spire was added to the church tower in 1808 to replace a leaded dome.

116. The village street of Shorwell, with its shop housed in a fine Georgian fronted building. On the right is the 'Five Bells Inn' in which, according to an 1879 advertisement "tourists will find comfortable accommodation, and where a week may be spent in exploring this picturesque neighbourhood". There was certainly plenty for them to see, including a fine church, three manor houses and the view from the Downs.

117. Wolverton Manor House was built in Elizabethan times by Sir John Dingley. In the 19th century it was a farmhouse and this rare interior photograph shows the hall of Thomas Carver's home. The two large pictures are of a Colonel Morgan and his sister. According to legend, there is a curse on whoever removes the two paintings from the house.

118. A typical Victorian farming scene, with an unknown farmer's wife milking the 'house' cow.

119, 120. A worker, posing with a straw hat and watch-chain, about to unload chalk on to the field at Calloway's Farm, Rockley in 1900, and carting corn in the Carisbrooke area.

121. Watering the horses after a day's work at Holden Farm, Roud.

122. A group of estate workers holding the tools of their trade: the gardener, a lady who is possibly in charge of the dairy, the general handyman, the mason or bricklayer, and finally the carpenter with his apron and rule.